W9-CTB-486

STEELHEADING
— FOR THE —
SIMPLE-MINDED
A BEGINNER'S GUIDE

by BOB ELLSBERG

Illustrations by Judith Tomlin
and Judy Hogan

Flying Pencil Publications
Portland, Oregon

Copyright © 1987 by Outdoor Enterprises.

All rights reserved. No part of this book may be reproduced in any manner whatsoever without prior written permission from the publisher except in the case of brief quotations embodied in critical reviews and articles. All inquiries should be addressed to Flying Pencil Publications, P.O. Box 19062, Portland, Oregon 97219.

First Edition, 1987
First Printing Published by Outdoor Enterprises

Second Printing, 1989
Published by Flying Pencil Publications
P.O. Box 19062
Portland, Oregon 97219

Manufactured in the United States of America

ISBN 0-916473-04-X

TABLE OF CONTENTS
Steelheading
for the Simple-minded

ACKNOWLEDGEMENTS

Writing and publishing a book, even if it is a labor of love, is very much a "labor." In my case, this effort was assisted by many good friends who love the sport and who supported my desire to share this love with you.

I would like to thank the staff of *The Daily Astorian*, who gave me my first opportunity to write about my outdoor experiences. Without their support and advice I would be an even rougher "diamond."

The friends who took the time to read my early efforts and to suggest necessary changes, and who provided encouragement when it was most needed, are greatly loved and appreciated.

A special thank you to my wife, Claudia, and son Steven, for being the subject of a few stories, and for allowing me the time to beat on the computer.

Finally, my most heartfelt thanks to Paul Barnum, who took the very rough work, used his considerable editing and writing skills, and made this book what I wanted it to be.

PREFACE

Entirely too many sports and outdoor activities get so involved in mystique and jargon that novices are discouraged from even trying. The purpose of this book is to entice the newcomer into giving steelhead fishing a shot.

To accomplish this goal, I have provided some information on the biology and habits of the fish, the equipment involved, and a few of the necessary techniques. Because fishing also involves sharing water with others, streamside etiquette and pointers on crowded fishing techniques are also explored.

The experience of steelheading is an exciting social and emotional phenomenon, so I have added a little "spice": stories and personal experiences that will give the novice a feel for the joy of the sport. My hope is that the reader, whether novice or lifelong steelheader, will use the information to develop their own store of tales. Reading others' observations is great, but there's no substitute like your own experience.

INTRODUCTION

This book is written to help you – the long-suffering fisherman – understand steelhead trout. It is dedicated to all those of us who love to pursue the challenge of ol' metalhead.

Of all the fish that suck water, steelhead must have the best press agent.

A mystical aura generally reserved for unicorns and mermaids surrounds this "legendary" fish. Most stories written about the sacred sea-going trout begin something like the following:

"After 15 days of unbelievable hardship we had almost given up hope. The freezing cold had taken its toll on flesh and spirit, but we trudged into the blizzard to make a few last casts."

With the scenario set, the writer hits us with the big moment.

"Peering up at my frozen rod tip through the falling snow, I saw the line stop, motionless in the rushing current. At that split-second, the water exploded and a giant flash of silver flew 10 feet into the air. My reel sang as the awesome fish bolted upstream. Fifty, 100 yards of line streamed off my spool. I gasped in wonder as the big fish cleared a 30-foot falls, made one more spectacular leap and then parted my line with a disdainful snap of its powerful head."

1

"Peering up at my frozen rod tip . . ."

That kind of writing sells copy, perhaps even a lot of it. But folks, I'm here to tell you. "It just ain't so!"

With good water conditions, a little luck, reasonably good equipment and a little understanding of your quarry, anyone can catch steelhead.

This book is dedicated to all who pursue the mighty "Salmo." May you have a thousand stories!

CHAPTER ONE
STEELHEAD:
THE FISH AND THE LEGEND

Steelhead! The legendary fighting fish of the Northwest. The mere mention of its name evokes visions of rushing green water thundering through stands of old growth fir. Fingers close around an imaginary reel, and ears ring with the scream of the racing drag as a leaping flash of silver is silhouetted against the stormy sky.

No doubt about it, steelhead have a great press agent. But deep down inside their little chromosomes, even a mighty 20-pounder is just an overgrown rainbow trout. That's right. That little 10-inch red-striped spotted rainbow you caught and released in the stream two years ago might have been that bright steelhead buck that broke your line last fall.

Rainbow trout (*oncorhynchus mykiss*) are a popular game fish that nature has distributed throughout Western America. Man, in an effort to do nature one better, has expanded the rainbows' range throughout the United States, South America, Europe, New Zealand and much of the civilized world.

Lakebound rainbows and those that spend their lives in freshwater streams generally have dark green backs and red lateral lines the length of their sides. A variety of black spots cover their bodies. This coloration serves to protect them in their native waters. These fish grow according to the food available and have been known to reach sizes of 10 pounds and more. When they mature at about three years of age, they spawn in the streams and tributaries of their home waters.

When rainbows have easy access to the ocean, however, they often enter the saltwater — most at 10 to 14 months at a length of about six to 10 inches. For the better part of the next two years they scatter widely and forage for food in the open ocean. During this sojourn they are transformed into a long sleek fish with a white belly, light silver sides and a gun metal grey coloring on their backs. This coloration provides protection from the various ocean predators and makes them look, at least in coloring, a great deal like the salmon that often frequent the same home streams. Their moniker, "steelhead," comes from the dark steel color of their head and back.

Steelhead tend to grow more rapidly than do their lake-bound brothers. A comparison of fish of equal weight would show the steelhead with a smaller head and a longer body than a lake fish. A fish's head grows at a constant rate. A fish with a large head in relation to its body has grown slowly. A relatively small head, like that of most steelhead, denotes more rapid growth.

Other trout, such as sea run cutthroat and German Brown, and various char species such as Dolly Varden, undergo a similar change in coloring when they enter saltwater.

Life is dangerous for the young steelhead in the ocean. Birds, seals and larger fish take a high toll, but those that survive grow quickly.

After two years in the ocean, bright steelhead generally return to the streams of their birth. This is not always the case. A very few strays go off course, but a good percentage of steelhead smolts — often as much as

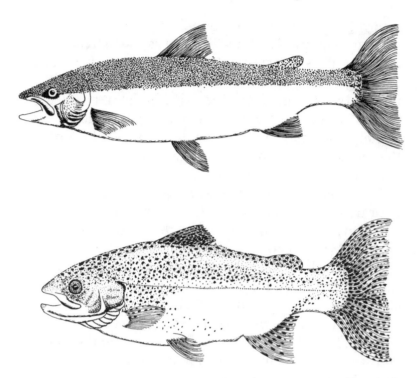

Rainbow Trout: Steelhead vs. Lakebound

Note the difference in coloring body shape and size of the two varieties of salmo gairdneri. *With different environmental conditions, one has spent its life in a lake while the other has had the opportunity to make it to the ocean. Both, however, are rainbow trout.*

10 percent – return home as mature fish to spawn and maintain the cycle.

The percentage of returning steelhead is much higher than that of salmon species, perhaps because of the lack of commercial fishing pressure on steelhead. Most fish return to their spawning grounds between early winter and early spring. Fresh water from rainfed streams entering the ocean seems the key to their upriver runs.

Fish generally migrate up river following the main flow of the stream. Often the fish will "hold" in still waters just off the main flow before scaling falls or long stretches of rapids. During the day, fish avoid waters that make them visible to predators, preferring waters at least three to four feet in depth.

As the fish enter the rivers and streams to spawn, their bodies metamorphose. Their silver sides darken as a red "spawning stripe" decorates the length of their bodies. The steel color of their dorsal area takes on a green hue. The fish quit feeding and their red flesh turns pale as nutrients are drained to develop the eggs and milt that fills their body cavities.

Once the fish reach their spawning grounds – gravel beds with swift water flows – they wait until their eggs and sperm ripen. Once ripe, a female digs her nest or "redd" in the gravel beds with her tail and deposits her eggs. The male, excited by her movements, releases a stream of milt that fertilizes her spawn. In a month and a half, the eggs hatch and the emergent small fry hide in the gravel, eating small insects and animals until they are big enough to start the cycle anew.

At least, that's the way nature planned it.

For more and more steelhead, the cycle is cut short. Long gone are the days of Romeo and Juliet steelhead. Man has taken control of the breeding process.

Fish on their spawning runs are intercepted in bins at hatcheries and are stripped of eggs and milt. Some hatcheries sacrifice the adults while others release the spawned-out fish back into the stream. Literally thousands of fish are processed in this fashion.

After fish have spawned, whether in the stream or at the hatchery, the survivors head for the ocean again. Most die in the passage. A few will make it back and return to spawn again a year later.

A fish that has been in the ocean two years is called a "two-salt fish." These fish are actually three years old, counting their "fry time." They weigh between six and 10 pounds and are between two and three feet in length. Those fish that return to spawn a second time or those that stay in the ocean for three years are known as "three-salt fish," and those that return after four years are "four-salt fish." A four-salt fish (actually five years old) is usually much larger than the more predominant three-year-old fish and may reach a weight of more than 20 pounds.

It's difficult to tell the difference between a hatchery-raised fish and a native. A few hatchery fish can be identified by the absence of the adipose fin, which hatchery workers clip before releasing the fish. Some have a microscopic wire with an imbedded stream code stuck into their snouts. But the most common way to tell the difference between a native and a hatchery-raised trout is to examine the dorsal fin.

Mature, native fish normally have high, arching, perfectly formed dorsals while the dorsals and other fins of the hatchery fish have been worn by the cement walls of the hatchery and by the gnawing teeth of fellow fingerlings.

Some fishermen claim they can tell a native by the fight or the coloration. You are best off to dismiss such rantings as fish stories. Look for clipped or worn fins.

Steelhead are now found in areas as remote as the Great Lakes and South America. The foremost areas in

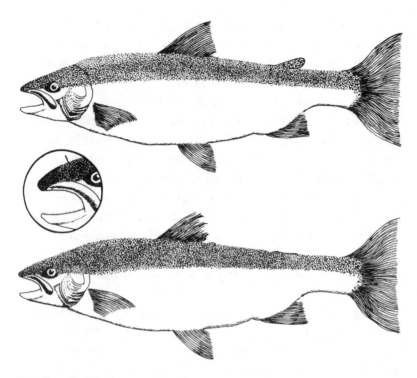

Steelhead: Native vs. Hatchery-raised

A native, stream-spawned fish has full fins (above), while a hatchery-raised specimen will have worn dorsals and a clipped adipose fin. The inset shows an example of a coded wire inserted in the fish's snout before release.

which to find old metalhead, however, are the streams of the Pacific Northwest.

On the West Coast, steelhead are present in coastal streams from the Sacramento River to the Arctic Circle. Fish have been found in streams as far south as Southern California, but rarely in fishable numbers.

While many fish hatch and spawn just a few miles from the ocean, some travel hundreds of miles up the Columbia, Sacramento and Frazier rivers to spawn in far away tributaries.

Some streams also provide good runs of summer steelhead. These fish are often much "fresher" than their winter counterparts and may wait several months to spawn. Entering the same streams as their cold-weather colleagues, they can provide a welcome addition to the runs of winter fish.

CHAPTER TWO
ROD AND REEL

Now that you know a little about its pedigree and lifestyle, how do you go about catching one of these elusive critters?

First you need a fishing rod and reel. Most fishermen prefer a long, eight to nine-foot rod. It should have good "feel," that indescribable quality that tells you whether your gear has run into a rock, a snag, or a fish. In addition, it should have a flexible tip and should be stout enough for you to put a little leverage on a big fish. Most rods have recommended line weights printed on their base. Six to 15-pound line is a good range for a steelhead rod.

The eyes or guides on the rod should be made of ceramic or of a tough metal. Steelhead put a lot of stress on the guides and can cause the line to wear through weak metal. Small diameter guides are made for use with casting reels while large guides are found on rods designed for spinning reels.

Many good fishermen make their own rods by first selecting "blank" rods and then attaching their own guides and reel mounts. This is the best way to go to get a rod tailored to your individual tastes.

The reel is the most critical piece of equipment you will purchase. In the past, most streamside fishermen used bail-type spinning reels. These are easy to cast and are excellent for use on small streams where short casts

Rod and Reel

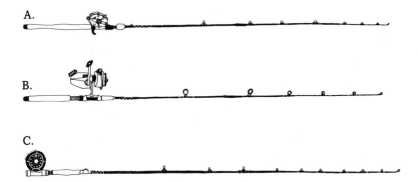

Steelhead fishing rods and reels

A. *Bait casting outfit*
B. *Spin casting outfit*
C. *Fly casting outfit*

with light weight are the rule. Most can be purchased at relatively low cost and have interchangeable spools.

These spinning reels work quite well and can last a fisherman many seasons. Typical problems are weak bail springs and angler-damaged handles, bails and spools. A fall can easily damage or break the exposed area of a spinning reel.

One morning, I got ambitious and took a three-hour hike to a favorite fishing hole on the Salmonberry River. While descending the slippery riprap I stumbled, fell and broke the base of my spinning reel, an inch above where it attached to the rod. I spent the rest of the day trying to cast with the broken reel in my left hand, my rod butt stuffed in my right arm pit, and working the bail with my right hand. Mercifully, I hooked no fish. Now I always carry a spare reel.

Many die-hard steelheaders are taking a lesson from bass fishermen and are switching to baitcasting reels.

These reels have long been the favorite of boat fishermen on large rivers. They hold more line, can take more of a beating, and allow the fisherman to use a lesser drag setting than is required with a spinning reel.

The disadvantage of baitcasting reels is that they take time to learn how to use, are difficult to cast with little weight, and they tend to backlash. A good baitcasting reel can cost more than $100. Some even come with "on board" computers that set drag and minimize backlash.

It took me two years to learn how to use my casting reel proficiently and I still backlash on occasion. Nothing is quite as exciting as the thrill of battling a big fish with a reel full of snarled line. I always carry two reels to the stream, and count on untangling major "bird nests" back home when my fingers have thawed.

While a fisherman can use a spinning rod with a baitcasting reel, most use a baitcasting rod. The blank is the same, but the guides are of a smaller diameter closer to the reel. A spinning rod, on the other hand, must accommodate a much steeper angle from the spool to the first guide, necessitating the guide's larger diameter.

Steelheaders who want the ultimate challenge try to take the big trout on flyrod and reel. A fly rod is generally longer than most casting or spinning rods and is more flexible. Fly reels are designed so that line is played out or retrieved by hand.

Unlike casting and spinning outfits, fly casting setups rely on the weight of the line for casting distance. This can provide a real advantage when one wishes to present a surface fly or bug to a feeding fish. Much of the advantage is lost, however, when the object is to get your gear to the bottom of a deep, rushing stream. Weighted flies and sinking line can aid the fly casting purist, but success comes only to the expert.

Baitcasting reel backlash

Fly fisherman and friends(?)

Fly fishing gear also proves impractical when fishing with a crowd of other anglers. Fly fishing requires a back cast and generally a different drift speed, factors which can make the fly angler highly unpopular with others fishing close to him.

A fly fisherman can gain some advantage fishing for steelhead during the summer or during the winter season on an uncrowded stream under low water conditions. Shy fish in exposed waters can be approached with a small fly presented with pinpoint accuracy and no splash. When hooked on fly tackle, a steelhead can provide a most remarkable experience and even more remarkable stories.

CHAPTER THREE

HOOK, LINE AND SINKER

To catch 'em, you first have to hook 'em

The most ancient of fishing equipment, common to prehistoric and primitive cultures, is the fish hook. First made of bone and wood, and later of a variety of metals and alloys, the hook serves one very basic function: to hold the fish onto the line. A sharp point drives the hook into the fish's mouth. In most cases, a barb on the hook's shaft prevents the hook from pulling loose.

A wide variety of hooks are currently used by steelhead fishermen. Preferred sizes may vary widely, from the relatively small #5 hook to the large 3/0 or even a 4/0.

All serve the purpose well. Size is really a matter of personal preference.

Many fishermen use hooks made of rustproof metal alloy. These work great, especially for those of us who forget and leave wet hooks in our tackle boxes. Many more use brass hooks. These are easier to conceal in a glob of eggs or under the dressing of a fly. Brass hooks also hold their point longer.

Serious steelheaders take a hook sharpener to the stream and use it often. Dull hooks often miss gentler takes of a fish. To do it right, resharpen your hook after every fish caught and after every solid snag.

One of the best fishermen I know makes it a point to sandpaper the sides of his brass hooks and paint them

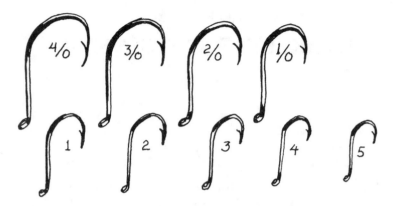

*Common hook sizes for steelhead fishing
(shown actual size)*

red. That makes sense. Fish strike at color. Why not improve your chances?

Those who like to release their fish will remove the barbs from their hooks. The practice generally doesn't result in losing any more fish, and it makes it easier to release a fish unharmed.

Testing line may be key to angling success

Novices and veterans alike ask themselves the question "What test line should I buy?"

Of course, there are as many answers as there are fishermen. The best way to approach this earth-shattering question is to remind yourself of the principles behind rod-and-reel fishing.

It's important to first understand the role fishing line plays in the big picture. Line connects the angler, via rod and reel, to the fish via lure or hook. Each line has a suggested test weight set in pounds. You set the reel's "drag" – or resistance to the line – at somewhat less than the line's breaking point. When a fish or the current applies more pressure than that set by the reel, the spool feeds out more line. As the fish changes direction – or tires – line can be retrieved, refilling the spool.

Fish are cold-blooded critters. Unlike a mammal, their blood and oxygen supply is quite limited. After a relatively quick fight, fish run out of oxygen, tire, and allow the angler to recover line and prize. If a fish had a mammal's staying power, line weights would have to be vastly increased and the fight would wear out most anglers.

A line is too light for the fish you are chasing if the fish can regularly run out your whole spool of line. You do have to put enough pressure on the line to stop or tire a fish within a reasonable distance and within a reasonable length of time.

A couple of summers ago, cutthroat trout fishermen using ultralight equipment with two-pound test "discovered" a large run of summer steelhead on a local stream. Although they had a great time hooking the fish, the tree-lined banks and snag-filled waters gave the big fish too much of an advantage. At the same time, line needed to stop a 10-pound steelhead would have been overkill for the 10-inch trout that were their primary quarry.

Another consideration is the terrain.

If you are fishing snag-free water, you can use a lighter line than if you are fishing water riddled with obstacles. The same applies if you are in a boat or have an open stream path in which to follow a fish. Given clear water, an angler can land a 40-pound chinook salmon on 10-pound test and really have a ball. If, however, the fishing grounds are snaggy or you can't follow a fish, it's best to use a much heftier line.

Sometimes, you have to "horse" a fish to shore. It's not as much fun as playing it to exhaustion, but some waters allow little choice.

There are many advantages to using light line. The lighter the test, the less visible the line. Those fish that spook at the sight of 12-pound line might not see six-pound test. Clearer water also may necessitate less visible line. You'll get more strikes, especially in clear water, with lighter line. It's easier to tie, requires less weight for a good drift and will provide many more yards of backup in the spool.

Most "break-offs" are not caused by too light a test but by line failure. In the heat of battle, line is nicked and scraped by rocks, snags and even the fish. As a chain is no stronger than its weakest link, so too is line no stronger than its weakest point. A good angler checks his line often and cuts off a few inches after he lands a fish to avoid future problems.

Snapped lines also result from tight or "sticky" drag on a reel. The drag should be set so that the spool gives out line easily, well below the line's breaking point. If the reel operates poorly, the power of an initial run or jump can bind the line and cause it to break. Heavier line does allow you to be less careful, but will cost you action and fish in the long run.

Different brands of line have different characteristics. Some lines tend to be stiff and difficult to cast. Others hold the spool's twist and are hard to break in. I prefer a relatively limp line that will not tangle easily.

Some lines are colored so that they are easily seen by anglers even in poor light. Others boast of their excellent invisible qualities. I would suggest that an angler not buy line in bulk until he can test a sample.

One year, I got carried away by a great bargain and ended up with 2,000 yards of garbage.

The next time your spool gets down to the critical level, or when you feel wealthy enough to afford a second spool, try lighter line. Give some thought to the waters you fish and the hazards you face. You should be able to make a choice that will bring you more fish and more fun.

Getting to the bottom of things

The most important rule of steelhead fishing is this: Get your hook to the bottom. A few varieties of spring and summer-run fish will take a surface fly, but the vast majority of steelhead only take baits and lures fished right down on the bottom.

Because most productive steelhead streams and rivers have fast and turbulent water, a fisherman must use a hefty amount of weight to counter stream flow and get his gear into proper position. Anglers solve this problem by using pieces of wire-like lead available in various diameters. Sold as either solid-core or hollow-core, the lead comes wound inside boxes or in packages of short lengths.

To attach the lead to his line, a fisherman can either crimp a hollow-core piece onto a piece of line near the swivel, or he can attach the lead to the line above the swivel using short pieces of surgical tubing. Most anglers attach the lead about 1½ to 3 feet above the hook.

The advantage of lead wire is that one can cut off different lengths to suit water depth, speed, and buoyancy problems with the bait and lure. The most common way of presenting bait to a fish is a slow drift

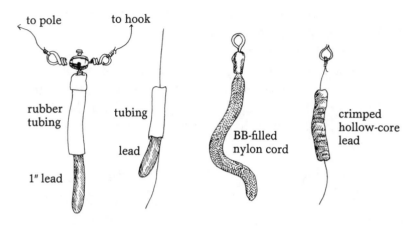

to pole   to hook

rubber
tubing   tubing

lead

BB-filled
nylon cord

crimped
hollow-core
lead

1" lead

Various weight setups for steelhead fishing

through a fast, deep run or a more placid hole. If you can't feel your gear bumping along the bottom, then you are probably not down deep enough and should use a longer length of lead. If your outfit sticks on the bottom with no movement, use a smaller length.

One problem with lead wire is that it tends to snag easily between rocks and in crevices. Using surgical tubing to hold the wire on the line alleviates this problem somewhat because the tubing can slide up and down the line and give some playing room. By using the hollow-core wire and crimping it onto the trail end of the leader, chances are the lead will just slide off the line and you'll at least preserve your terminal gear. Still another method is to attach the lead to a lighter test line than that used in the spool or for the leader. That way, when you break off, only the lead goes. This saves terminal gear, but takes time to tie up. Most steel-headers have resigned themselves to buying stock in sporting goods stores!

Some new gadgets show some promise. A weighted rubber ball serves as a substitute for lead wire. The ball is placed in the same location as the lead, often attached to a snap swivel a couple of feet above the bait or lure. Its round shape allows it to roll right over spots that ordinary lead might snag on. The balls are expensive, almost $1 a pop. They also makes a big splash when they hit the water.

More recently, lengths of nylon parachute cord filled with BBs have made their way into sporting goods stores. Attached to a snap swivel, and available in different lengths, the cord seems to resist snagging between rocks. It may be a good answer to the problem of how to keep tackle down without snagging up. These are easy to make. The do-it-yourselfer can save a lot of money putting together a supply of these weights.

Once you're finally on the bottom, a whole lot of things can entice a steelhead into striking. Although the fish do not feed at this life stage (I have yet to find anything other than eggs or milt in their body cavities), their feeding instinct seems to make them strike at "food," or anything closely related to food.

CHAPTER FOUR

BAIT AND LURES

Most steelhead bait and lures try to simulate the primary food sources of sea run rainbows. Young trout feed heavily on the eggs of salmonids and other fish that frequent their home rivers. Once the year-old trout enters saltwater, however, their diet leans heavily toward shrimp, krill and other crustaceans. After the fish enter their third year of life, small baitfish become a big part of their diet.

Even though winter steelhead are not eating when they travel upstream, their feeding instinct seems intact. Baits are used that imitate the trout's traditional bill of fare preferred in hungrier times.

One of the most common baits used throughout the steelhead's range are clusters of salmon or steelhead eggs. Eggs are held together in two tight skeins as a salmonid prepares to spawn. Connecting tissue breaks down just before spawning and the eggs separate. If a fish is caught while the skeins are still "tight," the two egg skeins are taken from the fish. These skeins may be cut into clusters the size of a quarter and "cured" in a mixture of borax, salt and sugar. Alum, jello and a variety of other ingredients also serve to preserve, toughen and color the eggs for use on the stream.

These clusters are then tied onto a hook that has been prepared with an egg "loop," simply a slip knot that will hold the egg cluster tight to the hook so it doesn't float

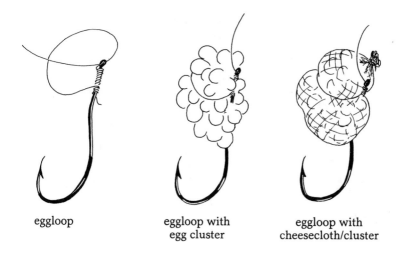

eggloop

eggloop with
egg cluster

eggloop with
cheesecloth/cluster

Examples of eggloops

away. The main problem with the bait is that it easily
falls off the hook. How to beat that problem is a puzzle
for anglers.

In Northern California, anglers wrap the clusters in
cheesecloth to form gauzy "berries." These covered eggs
hold together much better than exposed clusters and
seem to fool the fish just as well. Variations of the egg
loop described above also have varying success.

Anglers will add a strand of colored yarn to the tied
cluster. This yarn provides extra color and helps to hold
the cluster in the fish's mouth by catching strands of
yarn in the rows of teeth and gills.

Eggs can be expensive, are fragile, and make a mess.
They goop up your hands, clothing, rod and reel. As a
result, a number of suitable substitutes have been
developed.

The most common of these are baubles of plastic-
covered cork, called "corkies" or "okies" or "okie drifters."

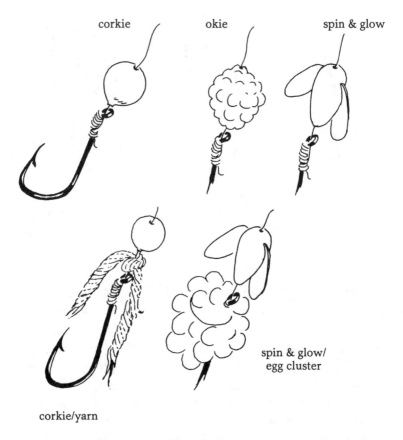

corkie   okie   spin & glow

spin & glow/
egg cluster

corkie/yarn

Common setups for steelhead fishing

These round, egg cluster-shaped lures are sometimes fixed with little wings which transform them into spinning torpedo shapes, called "spin 'n glows." They're offered in a variety of colors and sizes. A little hole in the center allows for threading onto the leader above the hook. These lures are often used with eggs to hold the clusters off the bottom of the stream.

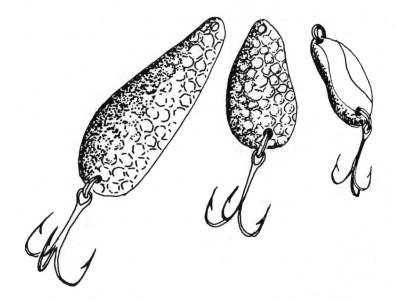

Spoons

Spinners

Many anglers use pink or green cork floats with a strand of yarn to simulate shrimp or other crustaceans. Various types of shrimp – mud shrimp, dried shrimp, and even prawns – are also used as suitable bait. Fancy flies can be tied to simulate shrimp and provide a flowing motion. Many steelhead waters are quite snaggy and all baits must be presented on the bottom, so most anglers avoid baits and lures that are expensive or take a lot of time to put together.

Hardware such as spoons, spinners, and plugs works well in many streams.

Spoons are especially effective in stretches of fast water. These heavy metal lures wobble enticingly along the bottom and can stimulate a resting fish into explosive action.

Still waters or deep pools are best worked with the variety of spinners made for steelhead fishing. Many have feathered hooks to simulate shrimp while others use orange beads to trigger the instinct to strike eggs.

The most popular lure used by those who fish larger rivers in drift boats are the floating plugs that dive and work the bottom when pulled against the current. The lures have a violent motion that excites fish into striking. Because they float, they tend to snag less often than the metal spoons and spinners used by most bank fishermen. Although they are quite expensive by steelheader standards, they are increasingly used by bank fishermen as well.

Other baits, such as nightcrawlers and crawfish, are used in different locales and almost any lure can prove successful given the right conditions. The most important consideration is that you use a bait or lure in which you have confidence and can work effectively, and which you don't mind sacrificing to the stream god.

Bait and Lures

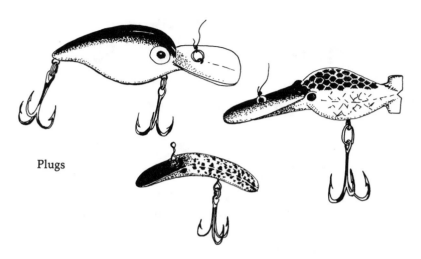

Plugs

Favorite steelhead fishing plugs

CHAPTER FIVE

DRESS FOR SUCCESS

Clothing makes the fisherman

Dress is as critical to a steelheader as it is to the fashion model. Under and outerwear provide the safety, comfort, and efficiency essential for challenging the winter streams and rivers.

Underwear – longjohns, woolies, thermals, etc. – should be worn in whatever numbers you find essential to combat the prevailing temperatures. Outerwear, however, is generally standard regardless of temperatures.

The key item in a steelheader's wardrobe is his footgear. Most steelheading, with the exception of spring or summer runs, involves wading, walking and just standing in ice cold water, which is often moving at or near flood speed.

Varieties of footgear include hip boots, waders, and sock waders worn under a pair of wading shoes. Whatever you wear, it is essential they fit well. I once borrowed a pair of waders a half-size too small. After 20 minutes in the water, my feet felt like they were set in concrete. On the other hand, boots that are too loose slip off your feet in the gooey mud often found along the river bank.

Shorter hip boots are commonly worn when fishing smaller streams or along the banks of larger rivers. More comfortable and lighter than waders, hip boots are much preferred when a good deal of climbing or hiking is required. They're a real relief when warmer weather dictates less rubber insulation.

A set of waders that covers the body from the feet to the armpits is a must if you plan to wade deep rivers or when treacherous waters need to be crossed. A good belt around the waist traps air in the waders and gives them some value as a flotation device – practical when the inevitable fall occurs. Water over your boot or wader tops, besides being very uncomfortable, makes a good anchor. An angler may find himself at the bottom of the stream for a permanent stay at steelhead level.

Some waders have boots built into the feet. Others just have smooth "socks" instead of boot bottoms. Tennis shoes or a good pair of wading boots are worn over these rubber socks.

Be sure to examine the tread. Will it hold on slick rocks and grip to mud? Some boots have deep rubber tread; others have a layer of felt designed to stick to moss and wet rock. Badly worn soles cause unnecessary slipping as well as bruised feet.

Some steelhead fishermen wear rain pants over their hip boots to provide further waterproofing. Most wear a knee-length waterproof rain jacket with a hood over their various shirts and sweaters. A good jacket has a lot of double-strength snaps and pockets with Velcro closures to store some of the gadgets, gear and tackle most fishermen pack to the stream.

Over this raincoat the diehard steelheader wears his piece-de-resistance: the fishing vest. Made of canvas or of some equally tough material, the vest is a patchwork of various-sized pockets embellished with ringed straps for tying on necessary gear. No vest ever has enough

Full hipboots make good anchors

pockets. The vest replaces most tackle boxes or most of the gear strewn on the bottom of a drift boat.

No well-dressed steelheader would consider approaching his quarry without a suitable fishing hat. Of value during any kind of weather, a hat is of vital importance, but it also makes a personal statement about yourself. On typical freezing days a good topper can keep in some 60 percent of the body heat lost through the head. On a sunny day, a good bill will keep out the glare and help an angler peer into the riffles. A good hat will keep the hail out of the eyes and deflect the stray alder branch.

Any design or style of hat is acceptable. But remember that your hat is the one feature other anglers will remember. Like a cattle brand, your hat becomes your distinguishing mark, the embodiment of your personality.

"See that fool in the red-and-blue fedora?" you'll hear someday. "He just broke off his fifth fish!"

Gimmicks and gadgets that can help

In addition to all of those baits, weights, line and tackle, all steelhead aficionados seem to savor the gadgets and gimmicks that sporting goods stores offer the willing consumer. Let me give you a rundown of a few of my favorites.

Most anglers need a pair of needle nose pliers to fix reels, squeeze hollow-core lead onto their line, and to cut lengths of weight. A set of handy pliers aid in releasing fish and removing hooks, and they also are good for extending your reach into creekbeds and up to high branches to retrieve the errant cast.

A deep net aids in getting fish out of drifts or holes hedged by deep banks or impassable rapids. A folding gaff helps to retrieve otherwise lost fish and it also helps when prying out lost gear and even dropped rods.

Small, round plastic boxes are now available to store prepared "setups" – the leaders and hooks dressed with cork and yarn that are the mainstay of most steelhead fishermen. Each box can handle a dozen or so setups, so at least two boxes are preferred.

All anglers need metal or plastic boxes in which to store spinners, spoons, lures and flies. These will also hold the essential peripherals such as pieces of surgical tubing, lead and hooks that easily get stuck in the bottom of pockets.

One item that will get a lot of use is a measuring tape

Overdressed steelheaders getting a lift

and scale combo. It will help to "de-lie" other anglers and will allow you to give an accurate account of the dark 20-pounder you chose to release.

Hook sharpeners are a must and can be kept with your fisherman's clipper and multi-function knife at the ready for a variety of emergencies.

Extra clothing and fingerless gloves for those really cold days are valuable things to pack along. Many anglers carry clamps or cleats that fit over waders or hip boots to give extra grip to the rocks. Fold-up walking sticks help in navigating slippery waters.

Steelhead are too big to fit into a creel or pouch, and razor sharp teeth and tough gills can tear up frozen fingers. A fish carrier made of wooden doweling is one of my most prized possessions.

Dress for Success

A pair of polarized glasses to spot fish through the glare are handy and, of course, you don't want to forget your fishing license and tag and a pen with which to record your catch. Finally, a good back-up reel and a small camera with extra lenses finish up the possessions of a well-equipped angler.

How do you get to the stream with all that gear? I'll let you know when I figure it out!

CHAPTER SIX

SIMPLE TECHNIQUES FOR THE SIMPLE-MINDED

Correctly reading the water is important

Equipped with rod and reel and various types of tackle, you are ready to hit the stream. There are basic tactics for catching the sea run rainbow that prove successful year after year.

Major variables to consider when fishing for steelhead are the size of the stream or river and the water condition of the stretch of river bank you are fishing.

Let's first explore the smaller streams. These waters, say, 10 to 20 feet in width, are among my favorite fishing venues. I'll generally use a spinning rod and reel because most casts are quite short. Lighter weight is the rule as the depth and current flow rarely require a lot of lead to get to the bottom of things.

A wise angler will go to his favorite little stream during the lowest water of the summer. This visit should provide a first hand look at the little holes, pockets of still water and long drifts that will hold fish during the turbulent winter flow. Keep in mind that these same waters will look much different after a heavy winter rain storm. It's best to identify some landmarks that you can associate with likely fishing spots.

Once the storms come, your first consideration is visibility. If you can't see at least six inches through the water, chances are that a fish's visibility is just as poor.

What they can't see, can't hurt them. Small streams tend to clear rapidly, but anything with less than six inches visibility is rarely worth trying.

During high water, fish move upstream all day long. Best spots are pools beneath small falls, long rapids and long slow drifts of relatively deep water. These are often found under a streamcut bank or downstream from a large boulder or submerged log.

It's best to use a little extra weight to get a slower drift and to leave the lure in front of the fish a little longer. In really murky water, I prefer a big glob of cluster eggs with a bit of bright red yarn. Fish see color, so show them plenty of it. Other good lures are larger size corkies and spin 'n glows.

I generally cast into the white water at the head of a hole or drift and let the outfit work along its entire length. Allow extra line to leave your reel at the cast and retrieve the slack until you can feel your outfit bobbing along the bottom. Slower waters beside a fast current are good bets. So is the tail of a pool.

In dirty water, spinners and other action lures are pretty much worthless. You may foul hook a fish but seldom will a fish react quickly enough to see and strike a fast-moving spinner or spoon.

If you catch a fish during high water conditions, keep working the same drift or hole. Fish are continually moving upstream and another fish will probably come along to replace the steelhead you just landed.

Low water changes the rules of the game. Small streams generally have little "holding" water. These are pockets deep enough for fish to rest in unseen, even during a bright, sunny day. Most upstream migration is during the hours of darkness, with little activity during daylight hours.

Smaller egg clusters and small cork lures or flies work well. Bright colors are no longer essential and greens and blues are popular. Flies also work well. Spinners, spoons and plugs are easily seen and can prove quite effective, especially in the deeper pockets and drifts.

During low water conditions, streams are best approached carefully and from downstream. The fish are moving upstream and will spook easily. Polarized glasses will enable you to see into the water, even during glare conditions. If you see fish before they see you, a carefully placed cast can result in a fish on.

Use as little weight as possible and cast well above a fish, allowing the bait or lure to work its way down to the fish. This natural approach, called the presentation, will likely not spook the wily steelie and enhance your chances of getting the river dweller to bite.

If no fish are seen in the pools and drifts, especially if water has been down for some time, it's best to try fast white water drifts, especially those with rock crevices or boulders near the bottom. Steelhead like the oxygen-rich riffles and will wedge themselves in between rocks for protection. I first dismissed these "white water" spots. But while diving to salvage gear a few years ago, I noticed that the white water stretches were full of fish working their way to the spawning grounds while the usual pools and pockets were bare.

During low water a pool or drift needs time to "rest" after a fish is fought or landed. Other fish in the hole will be disturbed by the action but generally calm down if left alone for a half-hour or so.

It is my experience that in streams with a hatchery, good high water fishing is found closer to the hatchery dam or ladder. During low water fish seem better distributed throughout the stream.

During extremely low water, fish congregate in one of two places: either in tidewater – the deeper, slower moving water near the mouth of the river – or at the confluence of two streams, for example, where a smaller stream runs into a larger one.

Larger streams or small rivers of 20 to 40 feet are best worked with bait casting rods and reels. These waters are often fished from boats and by anglers "plunking." This is "still fishing," where heavy weights hold the bait or line in one place. Fish are constantly moving in the big water, and the hope is that a fish will swim by and take the still bait. When plunking baits and lures, it's generally necessary to use a large bait or lure that spins in the current to get the attention of fish scattered throughout a large area.

Really large waters, those 60 feet to miles in width, are almost always "plunked." Anglers will use heavier gear than what they might use on smaller water. They're also likely to use rod holders and sit in chairs or fishing seats waiting for action. Fish tend to follow shorelines and are most often found within easy casting distance from shore. This kind of fishing is great family fun. Dad and mom can plunk and sit and sun, while the kids play in the sand under their parents' watchful gaze.

In some areas, ocean breakers near main rivers can be successfully worked to produce fish heading for the spawning grounds. Again, the water dwellers' propensity for following the shoreline works in the angler's favor.

Fishing a wide expanse of water calls for using an outfit with two baits. Just above a heavy sinker, attach a two-foot leader and hook primed with eggs, shrimp or other bait. A couple of feet above that, attach a swivel to which is connected a one-foot leader with a spinning lure. Fish tend to scatter in really large waters and the extra lure can pick up the action.

Distinguishing the bite from the bottom

You've done everything right: cast to the proper spot; attached enough weight to bounce along the bottom; and put on a tempting bait or lure. Now, how do you know when a fish strikes?

Contrary to popular opinion, most steelhead strikes are not of the arm wrecking variety. If you are drifting eggs, bait or some sort of lure, your first clue may well be that your drifting outfit stops dead in the water. Often a resting fish will take the bait or lure and gently hold it in its mouth. Many anglers jerk every time their outfit stops.

However, if the waters you are fishing have a lot of snags, jerking at every "pause" of the line can wear you down. On the other hand, if you are fishing a drift with a clean bottom, so that most of your drifts allow for a constant motion throughout the hole, a good hard set is worth trying if the line pauses at a point where it had moved freely before.

If your line heads upstream, that's the time to set the hook. Nothing but another angler snagging you will cause the upstream movement – nothing, that is, except ol' metalhead.

A gentle tapping, especially in a quiet hole, is cause for a solid jerk. It may be a small sculpin or trout but it could well be a much larger prize.

Often when steelhead fishing, your line will have a good deal of slack. If you set the hook with a good amount of loose line, even the most violent jerk will have little effect. If I have a big bow in my line, I'll set

the hook twice. Once right away, and a second set after
I've taken in the slack.

Sometimes, especially while you're fishing the tail end
of a drift, working a spinner or playing with a tight line,
a fish will strike powerfully and explosively. The
steelhead hits the hook and takes off downstream or
across the river.

The biggest mistake that even veterans make at this
point is forgetting to set the hook. This is not easy to do
when it's all you can do to hold onto the rod. You want
to believe that the fish is securely hooked. Don't be
fooled. The hook needs to be driven into the fish's
mouth and a hard, sharp motion is the solution.

Now that you have a fish hooked, what do you do?
Basically, playing a steelhead is similar to playing any
other good-sized fish. If your angling skills work for
bass, salmon, pike or walleye, they will put you in good
standing with steelhead.

A few things to remember are:

• keep the line tight. Slack line allows a fish to shake
loose or drop the hook;

• keep as short a distance as possible between you
and the fish. If it goes downstream or upstream, follow
it. A fish with a lot of line can work around stumps,
rocks and other snags easily. Besides, you get better feel
if you keep a "short rein" on the fish;

• don't get impatient. Wait until the fish is tired
before pulling it in toward the bank. Don't pull its head
out of the water. Without water to slow the motion of
the fish, they can easily spit out the hook.

• don't horse the fish in. Let it run up and down the
main channel until it's pooped, then slowly bring it in to

an available spot, preferably an unlittered, smooth bank with no visible roots or snags.

A couple of tricks may prove useful for special problems. If your fish gets around a root or snag, loosen your drag and let the fish run. After it tires you may be able to net it downstream, or you may be able to figure a way to free your line and retrieve line and fish.

Once, a nice hen snagged my line around a protruding root ball on the opposite side of the river. I gave line for several minutes until the fish tired. As the spent steelhead floated on its side downstream, a buddy netted my prize and removed my line so I could recover it from the twisted root ball.

When a hooked fish, especially a fresh one, takes off downstream through rapids, there is little you can do to stop its charge. If you put on pressure or tighten the drag, the fish will snap your line. Let the fish run and it will likely break the line off on the rocks. I've had a few run out my entire spool. Sometimes, if you throw your bail open or release your drag you can fool the fish. Once the pressure if off the hook, the fish will turn back upstream and swim back up to you. If nothing else, your effort will generally stop the fish and give you time to work your way downstream.

CHAPTER SEVEN

TRICKS OF THE TRADE

'Dirty' fishing holes require special tactics

Because I enjoy my rack time and tend to sleep in on occasion, I sometimes reach a fishing hole after it's been fished for quite a while and is "dirty" in my terminology. When you arrive at a dirty hole and want to pull a fish or two from its depths, you have to give some thought to a plan of attack.

If the water is high enough that fish are still moving upstream, you can do just what the successful streamside anglers are doing—mostly drifting eggs and corkies. But if the water is too low for fish to move—and if everyone has left—it's smart to use a few tricks of the trade.

I figure that any fish in the hole has had the traditional corky with yarn and eggs thrown its direction, probably to the point of boredom. Just to be sure, however, I'll generally try a couple of drifts with a corky to get a feel for the hole. Most anglers fish using just enough lead to get a smooth, slow drift along the bottom. Sometimes this method misses a few deep pockets where fish can lie. I'll use quite a bit of extra lead to search these hidden pockets. You lose a few outfits this way, but you hook a few more fish.

This method doesn't work when there's a line of fishermen, because you'll slow up everyone's fishing.

But when you get an abandoned dirty hole, it's a good thing to try.

Another tack is to work a spinner or spoon along the bottom. In a deep hole, put some lead a couple of feet above your gear. The early crowd can't use hardware because the angle necessary to work the gear would tangle the other lines. Something new in front of the fish works well, especially in low water. I'll use a spoon to fish fast-moving shallow holes; a spinner for slower, deeper pockets.

Shrimp or other exotic bait such as nightcrawlers often turn the trick. Many shops carry live sand shrimp. A buddy of mine in Alaska swears by freeze-dried shrimp. These dehydrated creatures are tough enough to hang on the hook and are a real attraction for salmon and steelhead. Most anglers don't use these baits, so again you are showing the fish something new.

Keep a supply of oddball-colored corkies and yarn. One year, there was a time when folks were killing steelhead on metallic blue corkies. Another time, my wife bought me a multicolored corky. I gave her a hard time about buying a "cute" color that no self-respecting fish would bite. I was down to my last setup one winter morning – the weird multicolored corky – so I decided to give it a try. Two casts netted two fish. I lost it shortly thereafter and have never found a suitable replacement.

Finally, look for those little pockets of water between the major holes that may have been overlooked. Often a fish or two are holding in these little drifts. I've hooked fish in holes with less than six square feet of surface water.

If you're a night owl and like to sleep in, you can expect to meet a crowd by the time you hit the stream. Remember that they are all fishermen, outdoorsmen and gentlemen like you. Enjoy their company, be polite and friendly and everyone can have a good time and catch fish. And remember, don't be afraid to challenge the "dirty" holes.

What's in a boat?

As more of our streams bear the omnipresent "NO TRESPASSING" sign, there will inevitably be an increase in the number of steelheaders using boats, rafts and other vessels to float through and fish the restricted waters.

Most boating is done on medium-sized rivers that offer enough water flow to easily float a small craft. The most common vessel is known as a "drift boat." These boats have a high arching bow for pushing through rough waters and a flat bottom that requires little water to keep it off the streambed.

Boats are "put in" at a public access dock or basin, drifted through restricted or inaccessible stretches of water, and "pulled out" at a downstream access point.

In many cases, the boats are just used as transportation. Inaccessible pockets or pools are stopping points, at which anglers tie up the boat and fish from shore. In especially rugged areas, some waters can only be reached by boat, allowing anglers to fish some great spots with no competition. Rafts, or any sort of small vessel, serve this purpose well.

Because of their maneuverability, drift boats offer a unique opportunity to work baits and lures in a fashion not possible for shore-bound anglers. Most boats are powered only by oars. When a good stretch of fishable water is approached, the guide or oar-pulling angler rows against the current while the other fishermen let

Working the current

their plugs and lures work near the bottom against the current.

This "back trolling" puts the moving lure in front of the fish for a long time and will often spur a fish into action. Many boat fishermen use this technique exclusively. Because most diving plugs work just above the bottom, very few are lost due to snagging. Baitcasting outfits hold up better under the constant working of lures and plugs, and are the preferred rod and reel of the boating set.

Boat fishermen also use the various types of bait and different setups plied by the bank angler. It is difficult to cover a fast drift as thoroughly from a boat as from the bank. Anglers will often beach a boat if they want to work a drift with baits.

A boat makes it much easier to chase a hooked fish and also allows the angler to use a somewhat lighter line. Fish can be netted from the boat, thus avoiding the shoreline rocks and roots that terrorize bank fishermen.

Etiquette demands that boat anglers carefully avoid interfering with those fishing from shore. Bank anglers tend to resent the advantage gained by "float fishermen," and get irate if drifting boats tangle lines and cause a shore angler to lose a fish. If you are lucky enough to be on a drift trip, you'll have plenty of waters to yourself. Respect those few pools worked by your shore-bound colleagues.

CHAPTER EIGHT

KEEP? OR CATCH 'N RELEASE?

A word about nets and gaffs

Once a fish is hooked and expertly played, it may be necessary to use a net or a gaff. Most experienced anglers prefer to beach their fish, looking for a shallow beach or gravel bar on which to guide the fish.

Some situations, however, preclude the possibility of landing a fish without some kind of mechanical assistance. Once, an out-of-town guest hooked his first steelhead in a deep pool just above a long stretch of rapids roaring through two steep cliff banks. After the fish took off downstream, the water flow was too fast to bring it back even after the fish had been exhausted. In order to get to the winded fish, I had to climb down a cliff above the rapids. Hanging out over the stream from a huckleberry bush, I finally netted the critter.

If you decide to use a net or gaff remember a few basic rules. First of all, don't grab onto either until the fish is ready to give up the war. Once you sacrifice one hand to hold a net or gaff, you instantly lose your concentration and your ability to chase the fish. Holding onto the net also leads to a desire to haul the fish in quickly, and frequently results in pulling out the hook or snapping the line.

When netting a fish I always net from the tail or downstream side. A net will spook a fish, so keep it out of its eyesight. If the fish takes a run, it will be forward

Taking one the hard way

or sideways – not backwards. If your net is below and behind the fish, you'll be okay, but if you try to net its head and the fish spooks, you may be in big trouble. Try not to touch the fish until the net has covered its entire length. Then lift quickly by pulling the net handle straight up. The net opening should be perpendicular to the water.

When netting a friend's fish, stay below the fish and try to stay to the bank side of the fish. If the fish takes off downstream, get back to shore. If the fish gets between you and the near bank, it's easy to get tangled with the line. Even a good buddy gets a little testy when you break off his prize fish.

Gaffs are bad news. They almost always will injure a fish, making later release impossible. In addition, they're diffficult to use with steelhead. The big trout are long and thin, and it's tough to stick a gaff hook through the body. Trying to get a gaff hook in the fish's mouth is no easy feat, either. In fact, a gaff becomes a great "de-hooker" if the fish decides to take off, or spins as the point reaches its mouth.

If I have to gaff a steelhead, I try to keep the fish facing away from the gaff and try to slide the gaff point inside the gill plate and out the mouth. Then I lift the fish to shore. I count on the fish spooking and bolting away a couple of times and am ready to toss the gaff out of the way if the fish requires more play.

How you can tell a 'good' fish

I readily confess to having a good bit of hunter-gatherer in my genes. If I catch fish, pick mushrooms or chase clams, I like to bring something home. I do release a few fish – mostly steelhead past their prime.

As an adult steelhead gets closer to spawning, its

48

value as food diminishes. Fat from its flesh is absorbed by the eggs and milt. Weeks of starvation deplete its system of nutrients, turning the ordinarily red meat to a yellowish white.

Few anglers want to keep a fish with no food value. Several clues tell you if a fish should be kept or released.

The first sign of a fish turning bad is its color. A really fresh fish is shiny, bright silver with a dark steel color down its back. These are called "mint bright" and should have excellent meat. After some "aging," a fish develops a red spawning stripe that runs lengthwise on each side. Fish lose their "shine" as scales are absorbed into the fish. Bellies darken and turn black. Finally, some fish get "rot spots" of white-colored fungus on them. At this point in their life cycle, resistance to disease is low.

Females can be identified by their mouths, which are more shallow-hinged than bucks, and their tail fins, which become worn when spawning. A hen's anal vent protrudes after she has spawned. Hens should not be kept if they have lost their "shine" and have already spawned.

Bucks will have red flesh and are edible despite a loss of color if they still have round, full bellies. Bucks are darker colored then hens, but as long as they are fat, they are probably good eating. In addition to more color, bucks can be identified by a much deeper jaw, which can develop a slight hook.

More anglers letting their quarry get away

An interesting and growing trend in the world of rod and reel is that of "catch and release." Every year, the fishing regulations list a few more areas dedicated to this type of angling.

49

The reasons for catch and release are varied. Some regulations protect fish populations threatened by low numbers of spawning stock.

On streams inhabited by protected steelhead, for example, only fish with the distinctive clipped fin from a hatchery can be taken; unclipped native fish must be released. As a matter of statewide policy, the Department of Fish and Wildlife in Oregon encourages fishermen to release all wild steelhead in order to enhance the native runs.

Some streams offer limited reproduction opportunities and can't support an active fishery. They soon would be "fished out" if anglers kept their catch.

More often, however, stretches of streams and rivers are protected to allow anglers a taste of "how it once was" and to allow them to try more challenging angling techniques, such as fly fishing or fishing with artificial lures. Fishermen must use barbless hooks and release all fish.

Some anglers are strictly catch and release fishermen. No matter what they catch, it is promptly returned to the water. Some don't eat fish; others believe they are saving declining populations.

These anglers are more than welcome to practice their habit, as long as they don't give me a dirty look on those rare times when I catch a fish!

Most fish and game biologists recommend the practice of releasing wild game fish, but you must do so before a daily or possession limit is taken. If the fish are handled carefully, they'll live to spawn and produce future generations of native fish.

If you plan to release, use a small barbless hook, avoid handling and ease the fish into the water. Don't touch the gills or squeeze the fish. It's best to leave the fish in the water and use a pair of needlenose pliers or a hook extractor to remove the hook. If the fish has swallowed the hook, cut the leader. Never throw or toss a fish back into the water. You could damage it internally. Instead, revive the fish by gently holding it upright in the stream, allowing the current to flow into its mouth, until the fish is able to swim away.

CHAPTER NINE

STREAMSIDE ETIQUETTE

Don't ruin another fisherman's big moment

When the fisherman goes off to the wild, he looks for many different things. Some look for the beauty of nature, others long for the challenge of pursuing the wily steelhead. Most welcome the opportunity to get away from the stress and pressure of everyday life. No one, to my knowledge, goes out expecting some rude interloper to raise his blood pressure and ruin his day.

Everyone has horror stories of fishing trips ruined by inconsiderate or unthinking individuals. Those who are intentionally rude won't have their behavior changed by any amount of education (short of a cedar post to the forehead). There is, however, a group of novices, who because of their inexperience and overexuberance, can spoil the fun for others.

Generally, fishermen go to the stream to get away from it all, not always to have a peaceful experience, but at least to yell at the fish alone. When approaching a fisherman working a particular drift, certain behaviors are positive and others are to be avoided.

Most fishermen approach another with the question, "How's it going? Any luck?" or some similar greeting. The response to this query will give you some idea of the angler's state of mind.

As a rule, I never fish a hole occupied by a single angler if other fishable areas are available. If the stream

Fishin' the line

is packed, it is best to pick a spot near the tail end of the hole or drift.

Fishing the "line" – tips for crowded waters

Long lines in America are a fact of life. We wait in line at the gas pump, the bank, at the show, and at the hamburger stand. So why, you may ask, would anyone want to stand at the end of a line of fisherman on a beautiful stream to catch a steelhead?

As long as fish swim upriver to spawn, scores of fishermen will line the stream to catch them. Two assumptions hold true whenever you see anglers fishing shoulder to shoulder. First, there's a good run of fish and second, the area in question is a good place to pursue them.

The advantages of joining the "steelhead line" are that you'll probably get to see a lot of fish caught; you will have a pretty good chance of hauling in one yourself; and you will learn a lot about fish behavior in that particular stretch of stream. The disadvantage of fishing in a line of competitors is that you must substantially modify your usual fishing techniques.

A lot of people can share a small stretch of river with little conflict if they follow certain rules of the stream.

The first rule involves position. If you get to the water well before daylight and are the first fool on the stream, you get your choice of spots. Everyone who arrives after you must take a position around you, giving you good working room until the crowd begins to gather. If you arrive at a hole after a crowd has already taken position on the line, you should try to find the least crowded position to set up shop. If folks are standing just a couple of feet apart, don't try to crowd in. Three feet on each side of an angler is about the minimum necessary to fish. If things are that tight by the time you arrive, you've overslept.

I always greet those already in place with some remark to let them know I'm sorry to be crowding their space. "Mind if I horn in on a few of your fish?" is a suitable salutation. Most folks know that you've got a right to fish and will adjust to your entry.

The major problem with crowded fishing holes is tangled line. Some tangles are inevitable, but you can avoid most of them if you follow a few common sense guidelines.

The first of these is to use the same amount of weight as those around you. If you use more weight, your gear will move too slowly and those upstream from you will run into your line. Use too light a weight and your line will run into those downstream from your cast.

When casting, always watch the anglers above you. Wait until their lines are in the water and are moving downstream. Then cast above their lines. Unless they snag – always a possibility – they should be well ahead of your outfit. When your line stops drifting, reel it in. If you troll the tail end of the drift, then those below you will snag your line.

If the water is flowing from right to left, cast backhand; from left to right, forehand. I generally step forward one-half of a step to get casting room and then step back into the line for my drift. Keep your rod at eye level or lower. If you fish with your rod high in the air, those fellows downstream won't be able to cast over your rod.

Don't move further into the stream than those fishing below you. It's impossible to get a good drift if some fool is out in the middle of the stream. You can't get a good cast and your line will drift right into his waders. It makes no difference where in the stream the "steelhead line" stands, but those in the line must keep a straight row.

When someone else hooks a fish, reel in your line – pronto! If you snag, break off your line. Don't cast again until the fish vacates the premises or is landed. If I'm in the water when a fish is hooked, I generally move close to the shore to allow the lucky angler room to chase the fish.

When an angler leaves to land a fish or change his setup, it's okay to edge over into his spot. But when he returns, you should resume your original position. As people limit or leave, those next door get first shot at their slots, but if no one moves over, feel free to move in yourself.

Like most crowded situations, things can get sticky if folks aren't considerate or don't cooperate. But if you respect the other fishermen, cheer their successes and follow these few guidelines, you can enjoy a "day on the line" with a lot of action and camaraderie.

Several years ago, on the Trask River near Tillamook, I fished a stretch of water where competition for chinook was so intense that fishermen practically cheered when others lost fish and cleared the hole. One old fellow in his 80s hooked a fish that he couldn't budge. A number of impatient anglers tried to convince him that he was snagged and that he should break off his line so that they could get on with their fishing. Half an hour later, the old gentleman landed a 54-pound King. Some snag.

Finally, don't help land a fish without the angler's consent. I get excited and love to get into the act, but many fishermen don't appreciate "help." Some like to beach a fish without the use of a net or a gaff. They like all the play from a fish they can get. Some fishermen will want to release an unwanted fish and don't want it injured.

One year on a coastal stream outside Astoria, I was reeling in an old "tule" chinook. The fish was so old it had rotten spots on its body. As I was bringing him in to release, a youngster who had been fishing downstream bounded over, gaffed the fish, pulled it ashore and clubbed it before I could utter a protest. He was so pleased to help that I couldn't get upset with him.

I really had no desire to take home a "fertilizer" fish and was especially displeased since the old "tule" filled my limit.

CHAPTER TEN

MISTAKES, MISHAPS AND MAYHEM

Attention to detail, including fishing regulations, is a sure way to make your fishing trips more enjoyable – both for yourself and for others.

Steelheading certainly isn't just for the neat and tidy. At least that's not the way I fish. At the same time, there are some procedures and guidelines that one can follow in order to maximize enjoyment of the pursuit of old metalhead.

Attention to detail can make a difference

Those who know me best – and presumably love me, too – attribute my love for the outdoors to my sloppy nature. The outdoors is one of the few places where you can be accepted in your most worn, most dirty, most comfortable clothes. It's a place where I'm in my element.

Clothes in disarray, covered with mud – no matter. In fact, if your hair is neatly combed and your face clean shaven, you're somewhat suspect by others in the field, maybe even viewed as a "Flatlander."

While understandably an attraction to many of us, too great a passion for slovenliness can cost you dearly. Lack of attention to detail can surely affect your success, as measured by fish in the freezer. I'm afraid I'm my own worst enemy in this regard. Every year many good outdoor opportunities are lost because I'm just too lazy to do things right. But, we can learn from our mistakes.

Steelhead benefit most from my untidy ways. Almost without fail my last cast of the season results in a stubborn snag. To break off, I inevitably tighten the drag to test strength and pull until something gives. As a result, the overset drag is forgotten and I break off my first fish the next fall. As the fish goes downstream, my reel stays frozen. The snap of a line is not the happiest sound with which to start your season!

Of equal consequence is my love for old fishing line. Line that served me well in seasons past surely must still be good. I hate to relegate it to the waste basket. New line always unspools the wrong way and is never as good as the old stuff. Unfortunately, the old stuff gets nicked, scraped and stretched, and then it breaks.

Invariably, my reluctance to put on new line results in "fish on" – followed shortly by "fish off." I also tend to let the line run a little low. One year, I watched with horror as a big hen chinook emptied my half-full spool.

With the drag properly set and the line replaced, my life is next made miserable by the quality of my knots. A knot that is a cinch to tie at 50 degrees becomes impossible to tie when it's cold enough to freeze the water in your pole guides. I try to get by with four wraps instead of five, or I'm too lazy to attach a swivel. the result is a brief fight, a limp pole and a red face.

As the season progresses, most loss is caused by all the free tackle I collect. As water levels rise and fall, a virtual hardware store of tackle is to be found on the exposed streambed. Much of it was lost by careful fishermen who tie beautiful flies and egg loops and who have terrific setups for weights and swivels. Out of respect for their art, I generally jam the gear into my

Streamside salvage

vest without checking knots or attaching new leader. Unfortunately, outfits that have been pre-stressed and beaten around the rocks for a few weeks lose a lot of their integrity.

One day, after a good week of salvage, I went to the local stream to work a freshet. There were wall-to-wall fishermen, but I found a spot and put on one of my newly acquired, previously owned outfits. My first cast was rewarded with a violent strike and an airborne monster that managed to break my golden oldie leader with one shake of its head. The gathered multitudes commiserated with my plight and went on with their efforts.

Just a fluke, I muttered, and tied on a second stream-seasoned outfit, this one a rubber corkie with a couple of good hooks. My second cast turned an eager steelie whose flight downstream was only barely interrupted by the snapping sound of my second-hand gear. By now, of course, the crowd was beginning to mumble.

This couldn't happen three times in a row, I reasoned. Undeterred, I put on a real beaut, a tri-colored fly with a lovely brass hook and a beautifully tied egg loop. My initial effort stopped and held halfway through the drift. I took in the slack and felt the motion of a swimming fish. A hard set put the fish into action. After five minutes, the fish caught its second wind and deftly parted the hook from its stream-beaten knot.

Woolen-clad colleagues by now were starting to point and snicker. Everyone's a critic, I thought, as I packed my gear and moved downstream to a more appreciative audience.

So, my fellow outdoorsmen, for your own enjoyment be casual, be sloppy, be loose – that's part of the fun of getting outdoors. Just don't set high expectations for yourself. You'll still have good stories, but you won't have to clean the fish.

Illegal techniques make trophies meaningless

Bragging forms as big a part of steelhead fishing as wet weather gear and numb fingers. The walls and desks of the Northwest are covered with snapshots of cheshire-smiling outdoorsmen hefting all kinds of finned creatures for visitors to ogle.

Among my mementos are shots of me as early as six months old, my grandfather comparing my length to that of a trophy chinook salmon. These are done in good fun and help us to recall old friends and happy moments.

Likewise, fishing stories form an important part of our culture. Put two longtime steelhead fishermen in the same room and soon they are sharing a wealth of outdoor lore. A good story well-told is almost as vivid an experience as being there.

These shared experiences create a wonderful data base unique to outdoorsmen. The fish may gain a few inches in the telling of the tale, but shared tips and observations on stream geography, fish habits, and latest catch information are valuable additions to a fisherman's store of fish facts.

Problems begin, however, when an outdoorsman's ego gets caught up in his hobby. If they are to be shared, woodland adventures should be a personal, exhilirating, honest experience. Things get out of hand when the teller expands the tale to inflate himself at the expense of others.

When success is measured in terms of trophies and meat on the table, problems befall the fisherman who feels he must out-perform his colleagues.

Not even the most skilled fisherman always "brings one home." Even the best get skunked some days. Luck is a critical element, an element that for most of us adds an exciting variable to our sport.

Those who get carried away by a need to produce game to sustain their self-image are forced to "give themselves an edge." Sometimes this edge is not that provided by years of experience, carefully chosen equipment and perserverance, but is that taken by playing loose with the rules and regulations that govern fishing.

To illustrate, several years ago a buddy and I fished a couple of good steelhead holes on the south fork of the Klaskanine River near the small Northwestern Oregon town of Olney. We were the first to visit the holes on that day and worked them thoroughly. After some time without any luck we hiked our way downstream to try a second pocket. Again we pulled a blank, so we walked back up to the rig.

As we arrived, two fishermen hiked up from the hole we had tried first. Both packed limits of nice steelhead. We swallowed our pride and asked how they had done so well.

"Well," said one of the anglers, "We use real light line, heavy sinkers, and have learned how to really fish the holes. We also have a special oil we use to cure our eggs." He went on to explain how he and his buddy knew the river and had fished steelhead since they were kids.

As you might guess, my friend and I started to do a slow burn. We were about ready to feed the two cocky "experts" a little steelhead sushi. But, after all, they had fish and we didn't, so we kept quiet.

After the pair left, we decided to give the hole a second try. As we approached, we found a broken line fouling the main drift. After some effort we snared the line and worked loose its terminal gear. The two "experts" had used 40-pound test line, six ounces of lead and 10-0 treble hooks – classic snagging gear. It would have been as sporting and as legal to blast the hole with dynamite!

The truly successful outdoorsman is the one who thoroughly enjoys the fishing and hunting experiencee regardless of outcome. The most successful are those who are respected and admired by those fortunate enough to share their trips. The very best are those who help others enjoy the joys of the wild.

The highest praise of all is that which comes from the novice, who, after spending happy hours learning from his teacher, tells others, "I never knew how much fun you can have fishing. My buddy really knows his stuff."

Trophies and meat in the freezer are not the ultimate marks of success. Don't be lured into giving up the joy of the outdoors if you fail to meet your expectations or those of others. At the same time, don't cheapen your experience by seeking the fleeting admiration of others for fish caught by bending the rules.

As the wise King Solomon advised, "Pride goes before destruction, and a haughty spirit before a fall." This holds for the streams as well as home and work.

How outdoorsmen can create some yesterdays

Can you name the best day of the week for the outdoorsman? Simple. It's "yesterday."

"You should have been here yesterday," is the classic chant after an unproductive day in the field, or by the stream, or on the ocean.

"Yesterday the bass hit anything you threw in the water. Yesterday the ducks came in to the decoys like long-lost brothers. Yesterday the clams showed everywhere. Yesterday the deer overran the clearcuts. Yesterday everybody limited."

None of us ever have enough yesterdays and most of us remember every one.

Yet, some people I encounter never seem to have any "yesterdays" worth recounting. Always unsuccessful, they're likely to claim a "providential hindrance" to their outdoor pursuits. No matter what the activity, they never have any luck.

Putting together some of their stories, I found a few key elements that seem to be responsible for their lamentable state. Let me offer you a few pointers that will help you to have a few more "yesterdays."

• Go fishing often. There is no substitute for experience. Good luck comes to those whose persistence gives them a chance to get the hang of things and improve their techniques.

• Spend a lot of time scouting. Do your scouting and preparation before you actually hit the stream. "Waste" a day scouting a stream during low water. Talk to the folks at the hatcheries and add to your store of information. Getting ready for the tomorrows is a good way to build some "yesterdays" into your life.

• Arrive early and leave late. During low water, it pays to be the first one to a hole. Take along a lunch and work a few holes in the afternoon. The fish have a second bite after the first wave of anglers leaves, and besides, the chores at home can wait another day!

Many people don't realize that many "yesterdays" either passed by before their todays began or didn't start until after they had left for home.

• Ask for advice. You may not be smarter than everyone else. The guy with all those fish is a good place to start. People at the sporting goods store often can give a you a good summary of techniques and results. A little time spent learning can take the place of a lot of experience.

A lot of "yesterdays" will be given to you if you take the time to ask questions and listen.

• Practice with and maintain your equipment. Test your rod and reel in the front yard. Tie some line to your kid's belt and have him run out the spool. It's a good way to check your drag and your line. Get into your waders and hose yourself off or step into a tub. Finding that leak isn't a fun surprise when you're 30 miles away from home and the water is 36 degrees.

Snapped line or frozen feet can turn a sure "yesterday" into a disaster.

• Don't break the laws to get your game. Don't give in to the temptation to snag a few steelhead if they're not biting. Cheating will diminish the glory of a "yesterday," one you may relive only with regret. True "yesterdays" are honest successes, ones you can brag about without guilt or shame.

Every outdoorsman lives with the hope that he will have a lot of "yesterdays" to remember and share with his friends. Follow the tips I listed and you may find that today will be the "yesterday" you'll fondly remember tomorrow.

CHAPTER ELEVEN
ALL IN THE FAMILY

The total experience of steelhead fishing is much more than a little biology, wet weather gear, rod and tackle, and a few angling techniques.

Most of the joy of pursuing the big trout comes from sharing the experience, the stories, the lies, and the disasters with family and friends. Shared experiences, whether triumphs or adversity, are some of the richest treasures of the outdoors.

Kids discover the flavor of the outdoors

Most parents try to pass on to their children those ideals, values and activities that have given them pleasure. Those who appreciate music spend hours teaching their youngsters about different instruments. They expose them to a variety of musical experiences.

Parents who love to ski will haul their diaper-clad offspring to the slopes at the first opportunity. Some of the more precocious may even break a leg or two before they are old enough for nursery school.

As you might guess by now, at our home the emphasis is on hunting, fishing and other sports. Our little guy was watching a boxing match within a half-hour of his hatching. By the time he was six-months old, Stevie had been elk hunting three or four times from a backpack and had an assist in catching a few cutthroat. His first word was not "mama" or "dada," but a most

A taste for the outdoors

appropriate "duck." He learned to set up his little yellow
rubber decoys in the bathtub in a perfect "J" pattern
while making all kinds of interesting duck calls.

Following the hunting tradition of our tribe, Stevie
had his picture taken on deer rugs, elk rugs and bobcat

67

hide. Trips to the country featured driving tours devoted to identifying various types of birds and mammals that populate our woods and waterways. With this background you might expect that my little scout has a well-developed appreciation for the great open spaces.

Not exactly.

My one-year-old is infatuated with the ecology of our area, all right, but only as food. That might be okay if we were talking about nuts and berries, fish or wild game. His tastes, however, run much more basic.

The first clue I had that something was amiss came on Stevie's first steelhead trip. After a substantial debate with the lad's overprotective mother on the merits of taking a rug-crawler out in 15-degree weather, I managed to loose my first-born from the apron strings. Bundled up like a sleeping bag with a face, Stevie nestled into my backpack and off we went.

Needless to say, the boy was delighted to be freed from the confines of our cozy home. He yelled and hollered with joy all the way to streamside. I explained all the fine points of tying gear and picking proper drifts. Stevie proved an attentive student.

For awhile, at least.

He drooled in awe as I showed him the proper way to unsnarl a backlash in a baitcasting reel. But as I demonstrated the technique for working a spinner into a deep pocket, I noticed a marked lack of comment from my protege. Assuming he was really getting interested, I showed him a few tricks necessary to retrieve a lure from a fir branch.

At that point, I heard a strange termite-like sound from behind my left ear. Craning over my shoulder, I saw my little woodsman making like a mountain beaver and chewing on a big alder branch. He had all the bark stripped and was happily whittling into the pulp with his four front teeth.

Of course, I avoided mentioning this embarrassment to his mother. Besides, she was too concerned about why his nose and fingers were still white to care about a few idiosyncracies.

An understanding spouse is the most important catch

An outdoorsman's most important and prized possession, his key to years of enjoyable hunting and fishing, is an understanding spouse. Without the love and support of this "significant other," you might as well use your fishing rods to hold up bean plants and relegate your rifle to a wall rack for ornamental purposes.

Despite all the strides women have made socially, politically and in every other field of endeavor, it is still rare to see a woman on a stream or in the woods. For some reason, which I don't claim to understand, outdoor pursuits like fishing and hunting remain the domain of the male. So, if you plan to frequent the outdoors – and you happen to be married – you need an understanding wife.

Rarely does a week go by that I don't run into a would-be outdoorsman crying the blues. "I used to hunt a lot when I was a kid," they cry. "But now my wife won't let me go out and shoot things." Or, "Yeah, I'd love to get out and catch a steelhead, but my wife wants me home weekends."

Most of these complainers are just looking for an available excuse to bow out of any outdoor activites. They would rather frequent a couch than a duck blind and only like ice when it's found cooling a six-pack. For

Homecoming...

a few, however, the problem of marital desertion is very real.

If your wife is against your hunting or fishing, stay home. Life's too short to spend it arguing. Nothing takes the fun out of a great morning on the stream like

All in the Family

"Whaddya expect me to do with that slimy thing?" Many a great hunt is erased from memory by such comments as "You can take that bloody thing somewhere else and clean it. . .and don't expect me to cook that stuff. . .and you'd better be out of those clothes before you step into this house!"

Whew.

Once a fishing buddy came to me with a problem. His girlfriend didn't like him spending time on the river with his pals. Would marriage cure this jealousy, he inquired?

I'm not a marriage counselor. In fact, it's all I can do to manage my own behavior. But I have yet to see a spouse get less demanding after tying the knot, and that works both ways. I advised my young friend to prepare himself to trade his four-wheel drive for a station wagon and to sell his tackle to pay for the phone bills to the in-laws. He eventually found another girlfriend – one who does like to fish.

Outdoor pursuits, like fitness activities, are often selfish endeavors. They take you away from family, stop you from completing household chores and keep you from other "productive" work. Like exercise, however, outdoor activity promotes good mental health and calms tensions caused by a long work week.

The best solution is to find a partner who enjoys the outdoors as much as you do. Many women love to hike and camp. Most enjoy outdoor sports. But the woman who enjoys these activities and who likes the rigors and excitement of pursuing fish and game with her mate is indeed a rare prize. A father who takes the time to share his outdoor expertise with his daughter may be doing a service to several generations of outdoorsmen.

The next best partner, in my opinion, is one who

understands her mate's need to get outdoors to fish and hunt. Most women face enough suffering in childbirth, so it's not surprising that the subtle "joys" of huddling inside a duck blind or wading a freezing steelhead stream don't appeal to them. They choose not to participate and find other activities they enjoy in your absence (with other women, you hope!)

All of my fishing and hunting buddies have wives who fall into the "supporting" category. They tell me that over the years they have reached "understandings" and have learned to "bargain" for outdoor time. For example, a visit to the in-laws is equal to a special hunt in Montana. A new pair of shoes is equal to a new set of waders. Doing the wash buys a couple of hours of stream time.

A different tack is to teach your wife to hunt and fish. In my own case, my wife is a good hunter and is quite skilled with a rod and reel. She will, however, tell all who will listen (and unfortunately, there are many) that I am an impossible teacher. To hear her tell it, all I do is yammer and yell. I admit I do get excited, especially when she ties into a good steelhead, but I've convinced myself that she needs the advice.

I did observe one time a classic example of how not to teach your beloved. A few years back, a friend and I went fishing with our wives in Alaska. The pink salmon were running and we set out in a small boat to catch a few. My friend's spouse confessed she hadn't fished in years. After a few moments, I could see that she had abandoned rod and reel for the sake of domestic tranquility.

Despite her reasonably good angling skills, my friend had advice and criticism for her "benefit" at every cast.

Finally, after an hour of "Howard Cosell" lambasting her every move, the good woman called it quits.

After the trip, I whispered to my wife that I couldn't believe how poorly my friend had behaved. "Yeah," she replied. "He must have taken lessons from you!"

Take my advice, have a buddy teach your wife those outdoor skills you want her to learn. He'll be more patient, more credible, and more forgiving. And he'll keep you on the stream during the day and off the couch at night!

Fishing buddy a rare find

One of the greatest blessings an outdoorsman can have is a good fishing buddy. Any good friend is a treasure, of course, but a fishing buddy is a special sort of critter. In my lifetime, I've had maybe three or four and I consider myself extremely fortunate.

Many people enjoy the solitude of the stream. It is, however, unwise and unsafe to do much "lone wolfing." I've dumped trucks into falls and stepped into yellow jacket nests. I know the value of ready help. When things go well, having some help to net the steelhead that's tangled your line around an old stump is invaluable.

Just as all acquaintances aren't classified as friends, all those who accompany you on a trip to the stream aren't real fishing buddies. After giving it a great deal of thought, I've come up with my set of standards for what I'd call a "great" fishing buddy.

• A fishing buddy has to share your level of enthusiasm for the sport. He or she doesn't have to be a fanatic if you aren't. But if you're the type who just has to be on the stream every day of the season, your buddy should share that dedication. If you only fish the first weekend in December and your buddy does the same, great. Your interest levels are similar and your relationship is solid.

• A good fishing buddy shares your outdoors ethics and philosophy. If you're a catch and release fisherman and your buddy is a meat hunter, the relationship is doomed. It's rough to share your excitement over fishing cutthroat on a hand-tied fly if your partner is drowning suckerbait, worms and eggs upstream. Likewise, if one of you is a firm believer in game laws and the other plays it fast and loose with the rules, conflict is inevitable.

I know people who won't let their children hunt or fish with certain people. They don't want their kids to pick up questionable outdoors habits. Obviously, such a person won't qualify as your fishing buddy.

• A fishing buddy must share your level of competence. I certainly believe in the master-novice relationship, but a buddy is most often an equal.

The relationship between fishing buddies is based on mutual respect for many things, but especially those skills in recognizing fishable water, determining which tackle to use, and playing hooked fish. Like most friendships, there will be strengths and weaknesses on both sides, but all in all, each will be similar in competence. Actually, if interest and stream time are equal, skill level generally irons out. In addition, you teach each other and share information, making you both better outdoorsmen.

• A fishing buddy never lies to you. This may seem strange, given the frequent exaggeration by fishermen, but truth between buddies is essential for two reasons. First, most successful outings are built on information gathered during less successful ones. If you receive bad intelligence, you are likely to waste your next time out working an empty stretch of stream. The most important value in being able to trust your buddy is that you can enjoy his experiences as much as he did. A good buddy gets as much pleasure (or pain) out of your stories as you do.

A few years ago, I spent some time fishing and hunting with a fellow who thought he had to lie about his forays into the wilds. He was always "just missing" a shot or "breaking off" a steelhead on the rocks. Finally, I noticed the facts weren't jibing and discovered he was lying to cover his lack of effort and skill. Suddenly, it was no fun talking to him about the outdoors. I couldn't share the joy of discovery with him.

• A good fishing buddy will sacrifice his "maybe" for your "sure thing." He gets as much joy out of your success as you do and extols your prowess to doubters when you aren't there to defend yourself.

This special friend will carefully explain to your wife why you need a new Gore-Tex duck jacket and four steelhead rods, and why all good archers need expensive arrows. He won't tell her how you nearly ran the truck off a cliff, fell in the deepest hole in the river, or almost got run over by a sow bear with two cubs.

• Finally, a good fishing buddy will try to understand why you gaffed his line instead of the fish and why you sent him through the devil's club and vinemaple and then forgot where you were supposed to pick him up. He laughs about the time his prize steelhead got left in your smoker for a whole week and ended up ashes.

A fishing buddy is someone special. If you're fortunate enough to have one, buy him lunch tomorrow. You're both lucky.

CHAPTER TWELVE

GREAT MOMENTS IN STEELHEADING

The next best thing to catching steelhead is telling stories about catching steelhead. It seems that wherever steelhead fishermen gather, there are yarns to spin and tales to weave. If steelheaders could somehow transfer the energy in tale telling into quilt making the way some women do, we could easily coat the earth several times over.

Probably every steelheader can say with Jackie Gleason, "I've got a million of 'em." Here's three of my favorites.

First fish is something special

Thanksgiving marks the unofficial start of the steelhead season, and given good rains steelhead will fill the streams by mid-December. That enigmatic first fish is generally available from mid-October on and always makes its captor feel smart, lucky and ready for the rest of the season. A good fisherman may catch a dozen or more fish every season, but that first one is something special.

Not all first fish are caught, of course. And for some reason, it seems like we always remember best the one that got away.

I'll never forget one early November morning. I had broke out my mothballed steelhead tackle for an early attempt on the stream. The water looked perfect – a

First loss of the season

little high but clear enough to work a lure. Miraculously, the stream bank held no competing anglers. You could tell this was the "window" between seasons.

The first few casts made me feel glad I was alone. Old line, reel-shaped from the long off-season in my garage, took some work before I could cast without backlash. It took several efforts, but eventually I was able to hit the water.

Fish definitely were in residence.

A silver spoon was jerked and dropped. A spinner was hit and after a brief battle, I landed a 3-pound jack silver salmon, still bright. It would provide a good meal. An old, red-backed adult took an orange spoon and gave a good tussle before I released it.

The action slowed and I rethought my strategy. A corky and hook replaced the hardware and I looped a glob of eggs onto the hook.

No sooner had I cast the glob into some riffles above a deep rift when the line tightened and raced downstream. With all the reaction of a drunken snail, I watched it go, amazed at the fury of the assault. Finally, the realization struck — "Fish On!" I made a feeble set and the fish swam powerfully in the swift current. One last hard pull and the line went slack.

"Set the hook!" I yelled at the idiot holding my rod.

After relooping the eggs, I made a second cast. Unbelievably, the same thing occurred, only this time I reacted with a hard set and the hook stayed.

The fish dove deep and stayed there, practically anchoring itself to the bottom. I applied all the pressure my 10-pound test would allow, but the fish lay submerged, moving up and down in a 10-yard area.

Like any angler, I tried to picture what manner of beast occupied the business end of my leader. After about 15 minutes, I was willing to bet it was a stray chinook or a huge silver, possibly foul-hooked.

The fish charged toward me and rolled as it plowed upstream. All bets were off. A silver flash, a light red stripe and a wide tail left no doubt in my mind. It was a steelhead, the first one of the season. The fish was heavy and deep, one of the big ones that seem to come early. The hook felt solid, but I found myself anxious to bring the fish to shore. Landing that first fish is important.

I saw myself lugging it to a dozen doorsteps before I took it home to be photographed next to my one-year-old son. This would the last year he'd be shorter than my biggest fish.

Snapping back to reality, the fight was far from over. The big steelie seemed to get stronger as the battle wore on. After a lull, he headed downstream. The water was clear with no logs to offer him cover, but a few yards downstream was the "dead line," a cable strung tight across the creek designating private property. We fought down to the wire and made our stand.

The fish surfaced briefly in the narrow channel, his wide mouth open deep and white – a big buck! Unable to raise the rod tip above the taut cable between us, or to follow him onto forbidden turf, I tried to turn him upstream.

No luck. Still full of fight, the buck charged into the shallows taking the low-lying line into the rocks. The leader snapped, throwing the line back into my face. The fish swam away.

Some people take their loss with grace and style, but not me. I screamed, yelled, cussed and cried. It made no difference that the entire season lay ahead. The first fish was lost.

Secret spot

Search for the perfect steelhead hole

Some holes are so secret they're best left alone.
One weekend, a buddy and I trekked to one of those
secret holes. As a general rule, I am willing to freeze
when I'm fishing and to stumble through dense forest
only when I'm hunting. Little did I dream that on this
trip I'd get a good dose of both.

We left town in the general vicinity of the crack of
dawn and had a pleasant drive through the Lewis and
Clark Valley between Astoria and Seaside on the North
Oregon Coast. A good-sized herd of elk was out grazing,
but they got to the trees before we could get them on
film. We drove into the woods, parked by the side of
the road, and then followed a snow-covered trail down
to the river.

I had discovered this secret hole recently (known by
only, say 2,000 others) and was curious to give it a shot.
My fishing buddy was game, although he did balk when
I asked if he had a rope.

After falling into the river, smacking my elbow on the
bottom and floating my camera down a rapids, I
reached the entrance to the fabled spot. The ledge down
to the hole was narrow and slippery, offering a 15-foot
fall into about 20 feet of snow melt for those with
something less than goat-sure footwork.

Having no illusions about my ability to stand upright,
let alone climb rock, I had purloined about 70 feet of
half-inch crab line to aid the effort. We secured the line
to a stout alder well above the ledge and proceeded
gingerly across the rock face. The climb was a little
spooky, but the rope made it quite safe and offered a
nice "security blanket."

The water was beautiful, steelhead green, with about

81

three feet of visibility. Low water had bottled fish up at spots similar to this one, so I figured this would be a great morning.

Two hours and three inches of cold hail later, I began to lose faith. We had tried every trick either of us knew to no avail. The hail came down so heavy it drifted on our poles. We couldn't see our lines and rod tips. The water that seeped into my hip boots seemed to freeze solid around my toes. Feeling in my fingers, of course, had long since disappeared.

As an old steelheader, I figured things were just getting good, but my partner kept jabbering about frostbite and hypothermia and persuaded me to call it a day. Little did we know that our day was just beginning.

Hail had made the footing interesting. Three inches of the slick stuff doesn't do much to improve the friction between worn rubber boots and mossy rock. My partner's first effort to get up to the ledge produced a long fall and slide that left him prone and clawing at the frozen tundra, inches from the bank. A few millimeters more and he would have swam out. After a little more planning and a tighter grip on the rope, he pulled himself up hand over hand to the ledge and freedom.

Half an hour later, I was still flailing away, trying to climb up the frozen rock. Foremost among my discoveries was that half-inch line is too small for my giant paws to grip. And if you can't feel your fingers, you can't get a grip anyway. Also, ice-covered rock gets more slippery after several attempts to scale it.

There was no back entrance to this hole. It had to be up, up and away.

Finally, after debating the merits of rafting out. I persuaded my buddy into coming back out on the ledge to give me a hand. That was no small feat. I weigh a good 50-60 pounds more than he does and he was already on safe ground.

He was reluctant to venture back toward the pit trap, but I assured him that a dunking would be far superior to the wrath of the widow Ellsberg. Minutes — and gallons of adrenalin — later, we were out of the secret spot and had only a 200-foot climb up a frozen mountainside and a quarter mile hike back to the truck.

On our way back to town, we saw the rig of another fishing friend parked right next to the river with a cakewalk to streamside. He had hooked 12 before he called it a day and limited.

Generally, I don't give away my "secret spots," but listen. If you've got some rope . . .

This 'put-away day' was one to remember

"Put-away day" is one of those bittersweet benchmarks on my outdoors calendar. Waves of spawning fish enter our streams with the rains of August and provide months of excitement. With the emergence of spring, the last steelhead completes the mating cycle. Although the season is formally open until April, other commitments (wife, kids, job, etc.) conspire to retire my equipment sometime in early March.

After one last shot at the stream, the "put-away" ritual begins. Battered and abused reels are taken in for new parts and repair. Rods are cleaned, oiled and reglued. A few scraps of gear left from the small fortune invested during the season are relegated to the big tackle box for summer storage. The old vest is emptied and the fishing coat washed and rewashed in a vain attempt to remove the old dried salmon eggs from deep inside the pockets.

"Putaway" day

Waders are dried out, washed and repaired – their "foot-ripened" inserts ceremoniously burned.

One year, however, "put-away day" had even more significance than usual. This final foray to the spring-kissed stream also marked the last moments my fishing buddy, Mark, would spend as as an unmarried man. A longtime friend, Harry, had traveled from Idaho for the ceremony and joined us on our expedition. After giving Mark a thorough razzing about the possibilities of his "put-away day" being of a permanent nature, we drove out to the stream.

A perfectly good season that boasted days of snow, ice and frozen guides had degenerated into a warm,

84

sunny, beautiful day suitable for picnicking. The fishing, strangely enough, was terrific.

Harry took only three casts to beach a fat buck. A couple of hours later we had released several fish and had kept three bright orange-fleshed steelhead to be dispersed to the wedding guests.

Time was running short, and Mark started whimpering about getting back home in time for a shower before the festivities. In response, Harry went upstream to try "one more hole." I crossed the stream to get away from the whining bridegroom.

As seemed only fitting for a defeated bachelor, Mark hooked and fought his last fish – a fellow loser: an old, tired, sore-sided buck who looked little better than his captor. The fish was gingerly released to pursue his downstream journey.

My side of the river was one of those "suicide drifts" that no steelhead nut can resist. Although it allowed for great presentation, there was no way one could land a hooked fish. A steep six-foot bank fell into more than 10 feet of water. Below the bank was a huge log jam. And above the hole was a tangle of salmonberry and an undercut bank.

"If you hook one, I'll cast over and I'll reel your pole across," Mark suggested.

I laughed my reply just as my eggs were sucked under. My reel screamed as it grudgingly fed out line to a fish intent on taking the entire outfit upstream. Sighting up my line, I could see it disappear under a submerged log. I charged upstream into the brush and stepped off onto a partially submerged stump. The line rubbed against an unseen snag as the fish continued to tug away.

Mark was rolling with laughter on the far bank as I

leaned precariously out over the bank trying to free the line. The fish, which I had assumed was going upstream, had actually looped the line around a root ball and was heading seaward. After no small pains, I freed the line.

Mark regained his feet and shouted his support.

"I'll just cast across to you. Snag my lure on your pole and I'll haul it across," he yelled in excitement.

The fish hadn't surfaced yet, so I hollered back to Mark that we should look at it before we tried anything crazy. Just then the fish rolled, a bright silver hen.

Let the craziness begin!

I heard a whizzing sound next to my left ear and turned to find Mark's plug in a bush above me. After some effort, line and lure were secured to my outfit. Mark took in the slack and I pushed my favorite rod and reel gingerly into the green water. All went well for the first few feet. Mark reeled in his line and my pole drifted toward the opposite bank.

As soon as I scrambled out of the brush and headed downstream to a crossing point, all hell broke loose. The fish, tiring of our game, took off. My unsecured, unmanned pole fed out line to the untiring fish. Mark's reel sang as the weight of the fish and the drifting rod and reel strained his line dangerously close to the breaking point.

I screamed out unheard instructions as Mark fumbled with the gear. Finally, poles, fish, Mark and I met on an island in the middle of the rapids and together, we landed the fish.

Anything more would have been anticlimactic. Harry rejoined us and we packed up and headed home. We allowed just enough time for Mark to clean the fish, shower, and put on his white tux. His last "put-away day" as a single man would be one to remember.

ABOUT THE AUTHOR

Bob Ellsberg is irrepressible – a cascade of enthusiasm for his obsessions – fishing and hunting, storytelling, and teaching.

Born in California and educated near the rich waters of the Sacramento River, Bob was rarely far from a fishing rod. After a decade of public service as a police officer and teacher in the San Francisco Bay Area, he tired of the traffic and chaos, and headed for the more peaceful (and fishful) geography of Astoria in Northwest Oregon, where he lives with his wife, Claudia, and their two children.

In Oregon, Bob found he could blend his commitments to public service and the outdoors. He has conducted classes in fishing and in woodlands ecology for the Boy Scouts and for the Oregon Department of Fish and Wildlife. He serves on the Oregon State Parks Advisory Committee, and was Vice President of the Columbia River Estuary Task Force.

From his office at Clatsop Community College, where he is Director of Cooperative Education, Bob keeps an eye on the Mighty Columbia – inspiration for frequent fishing adventures, and for his weekly outdoors column for the *Daily Astorian*, "On the Outside." A selection of these columns, which have delighted Northwest readers with their humor and practial wisdom, grew into *Steelheading for the Simple-minded*.

Other Books by Bob Ellsberg:
Salmon Fishing for the Simple-minded

BOOKS TO HELP YOU PLAN YOUR STEELHEADING GET-AWAYS

FISHING IN OREGON
By Dan Casali and Madelynne Diness
Most Oregon anglers won't leave home without this detailed guide to over 1200 sport-fishing waters, including some of the nation's top steelhead rivers. It offers a wealth of maps, photos, descriptions, directions. "The best single source of information," says *Field & Stream.*
224 pp. paperback
$12.95

FISHING THE OREGON COUNTRY
by Francis Ames
Why stay put if the fishing's off? or pack up your rods when the 'season' ends? There's great fishing in Oregon the year around. Frank Ames tells you how to find it and fish it. "We know of no better introduction to Oregon sport-fishing," say *Fishing in Oregon* authors.
220 pp. paperback
$10.95

NORTHERN OREGON CASCADES Topographic Atlas
by Madelynne Diness
94 high quality b&w reproductions of USGS topo maps for one of the Northwest's most popular outdoor recreation areas. 11 x 14 format. Index to waters.
111 pp. paperback
$5.95

My check (or m.o.) for the following books is enclosed:

_____ FIO ($12.95) _____ FOC ($10.95) _____ TOPO ($5.95)

Add $2 shipping for one book, $1 for each additional book.

SHIP TO:

_____

_____

_____

FLYING PENCIL PUBLICATIONS
PO BOX 19062
Portland, OR 97219 Tel: (503) 245-2314